The Life of John D. Rockefeller

Biography of a Genius

Orison S. Marden

stanfordpub.com

Contents

JOHN D. ROCKEFELLER

THE richest man in the United States, John Davidson Rockefeller, has consented to break his rule never to talk for publication; and he has told me the story of his early struggles and triumphs, and given utterance to some strikingly interesting observations anent the same. In doing so, he was influenced by the argument that there is something of helpfulness, of inspiration, in the career of every self-made man.

While many such careers have been prolific of vivid contrasts, this one is simply marvelous. Whatever may be said by political economists of the dangers of vast aggregations of wealth in the hands of the few, there can be no question of the extraordinary interest attaching to the life story of a man who was a farm laborer at the age of fifteen, who left school at eighteen, because he felt it to be his duty to care for his mother and brother, and who, at the zenith of his business career, has endowed Chicago University with $7,500,000 out of a fortune estimated at over $300,000,000 —probably the largest single fortune on earth.

The story opens in a fertile valley in Tioga County, New York, near the village of Richford, where John D. Rockefeller was born on his father's farm in July, 1838. The parents of the boy were church-going, conscientious, debt-abhorring folk, who preferred the independence of a few acres to a mortgaged domain. They were Americans to the backbone, intelligent, industrious people, not very poor and certainly not very rich, for at fourteen John hired out to neighboring farmers during the summer months, in order to earn his way and not be dependent upon those he loved. His father was able to attend to the little farm himself, and thus it happened that the youth spent several summers away from home, toiling from sunrise to sunset, and sharing the humble life of the people he served.

HIS EARLY DREAM AND PURPOSE

Did the tired boy, peering from his attic window, ever dream of his future?

He said to a youthful companion of Richford, a farmer's boy like himself: "I would like to own all the land in this valley, as far as I can see. I sometimes dream of wealth and power. Do you think we shall ever be worth one hundred thousand dollars, you and I? I hope to,—some day."

Who can estimate the influence such a life as this must have had upon the future multi-millionaire? I asked Mr. Rockefeller about this, and found him enthusiastic over the advantages which he had received from his rural surroundings, and full of faith in the ability of the country boy to surpass his city cousin.

"To my mind," he said, "there is something unfortunate in being born in a city. Most young men raised in New York and other large centers have not had the struggles which come to us who were reared in the country. It is a noticeable fact that the country men are crowding out the city fellows who have wealthy fathers. They are willing to do more work and go through more for the sake of winning success in the end. Sons of wealthy parents haven't a ghost of a show in competition with the fellows who come from the country with a determination to do something in the world."

The next step in the young man's life was his going to Cleveland, Ohio, in his sixteenth year.

"That was a great change in my life," said he. "Going to Cleveland was my first experience in a great city, and I shall never forget those years. I began work there as an office-boy, and learned a great deal about business methods while filling that position. But what benefited me most in going to Cleveland was the new insight I gained as to what a great place the world really is. I had plenty of ambition then, and saw that, if I was to accomplish much, I would have to work very, very hard, indeed."

SCHOOL DAYS

He found time, during the year 1854, to attend the sessions of the school which is now known as the Central High School. It was a brick edifice, surrounded by grounds which contained a number of hickory trees. It has long since been superseded by a larger and handsomer building, but Andrew J. Freese, the teacher, is still living. It is one of the proudest recollections of this delightful old gentleman's life that John D. Rockefeller went to school with him. I visited him at his residence in Cleveland the other day, and he said:

"John was one of the best boys I had. He was always polite, but when the other boys threw hickory clubs at him, or attempted any undue familiarities with him, he would stop smiling and sail into them. Young Hanna—Marcus A. Hanna,—who was also a pupil, learned this, to his cost, more than once, and so did young Jones, the present Nevada senator. I have had several very distinguished pupils, you see, and one of my girls is now Mrs. John D. Rockefeller. I had Edward Wolcott, the Colorado senator, later on. Yes, John was about as intelligent and well-behaved a chap as I ever had. Here is one of his essays which you may copy, if you wish."

Mr. Rockefeller, I am quite sure, will pardon me for copying his composition at this late day, for its tone and subject matter reflect credit upon him:—

"Freedom is one of the most desirable of all blessings. Even the smallest bird or insect loves to be free. Take, for instance, a robin that has always been free to fly from tree to tree, and sing its cheerful song from day to day,— catch it, and put it into a cage which is to it nothing less than a prison, and, although it may be there tended with the choicest care, yet it is not content. How eloquently does it plead, though in silence, for liberty. From day to day it sits mournfully upon its perch, meditating, as it were, some way for its escape, and when at last this is effected, how cheerfully does it wing its way out from its gloomy prison-house to sing undisturbed in the branches of the first trees.

It was greatly to the regret of the teacher that John came to him one day to announce his purpose to leave school. Mr. Freese urged him to remain two years longer, in order that he might complete the course, but the young man told him he felt obliged to earn more money than he was getting, because of his desire to provide for his mother and brother. He had received an offer, he said, of a place on the freight docks as a bill clerk, and this job would take him away from his studies.

A RAFT OF HOOP POLES

A short time afterwards, when Mr. Freese visited his former pupil at the freight dock, he found the young man seated on a bale of goods, bill book and pencil in hand. Pointing to a raft of hoop poles in the water, John told his caller that he had purchased them from a Canadian who had brought them across Lake Erie, expecting to sell them. Failing in this, the owner gladly accepted a cash offer from young Rockefeller, who named a price below the usual market rates. The young man explained that he had saved a little money out of his wages, and that this was his first speculation. He afterwards told Mr. Freese that he rafted the purchase himself to a flour mill, and disposed of his bargain at a profit of fifty dollars.[1]

---

[1] This hoop pole story is matched by another, related by a friend, of Rockefeller's later warehouse days in

THE ODOR OF OIL

"There must be some way of deodorizing this oil," said John, "and I will find it. There ought to be a good sale for it for illuminating purposes, if the good oil can be separated from the sediment, and that awful smell gotten rid of."

How well the young man profited by the accidental meeting is a matter of history. But I am digressing.

Cleveland. He one day bought a lot of beans. He bought them cheap, because they were damaged. Instead of selling them at a slight advance, as most dealers would have done, he spent all his spare time, for weeks, in the attic of his warehouse, sorting over those beans. He took out all the blackened and injured ones, and in the end he got a fancy price for the remainder, because they were of extra quality.

HIS FIRST LEDGER, AND THE ITEMS IN IT

While in Cleveland, slaving away at his tasks, Mr. Rockefeller was training himself for the more busy days to come. He kept a small ledger in which he entered all his receipts and expenditures, and I had the privilege of examining this interesting little book, and having its contents explained to me. It was nothing more than a small, paper-backed memorandum book.

"When I looked this book up the other day, I thought I had but the cover," said Mr. Rockefeller, "but, on examination, I perceived that I had utilized the cover to write on. In those days I was very economical, just as I am economical now. Economy is a virtue. I hadn't seen my little ledger for a long time, when I found it among some old things. It is more than forty-two years ago since I wrote what it contains. I called it 'Ledger A,' and I wouldn't exchange it now for all the ledgers in New York city and their contents. A glance through it shows me how carefully I kept account of my receipts and disbursements. I only wish more young men could be induced to keep accounts like this nowadays. It would go far toward teaching them the value of money.

"Every young man should take care of his money. I think it is a man's duty to make all the money he can, keep all he can, and give away all he can. I have followed this principle religiously all my life, as is evidenced in this book. It tells me just what I did with my money during my first few years in business. Between September, 1855, and January, 1856, I received just fifty dollars. Out of this sum I paid for my washing and my board, and managed to save a little besides. I find, in looking through the book, that I gave a cent to Sunday school every Sunday. It wasn't much, but it was all that I could afford to give to that particular object. What I could afford to give to the various religious and charitable works, I gave regularly. It is a good habit for a young man to get into.

"During my second year in Cleveland, I earned twenty-five dollars a month. I was beginning to be a capitalist," said Mr. Rockefeller, "and I suppose I ought to have considered myself a criminal for having so much money. I paid all my own bills at this time, and had some money to give away. I also had the happiness of saving some. I am not sure, but I was more independent then than now. I couldn't buy the most fashionable cut of clothing, but I dressed well enough. I certainly did not buy any clothes I couldn't pay for, as some young men do that I know of. I didn't make any obligations I could not meet, and my earnest advice is for every young man to live within his means. One of the swiftest 'toboggan slides' I know of, is for a young fellow just starting out into the world to go into debt.

"During the time between November, 1855, and April, 1856, I paid out just nine dollars and nine cents for clothing. And there is one item that was certainly extravagant as I usually wore mittens in the winter. This item is for fur gloves, two dollars and a half. In this same period, I gave away five dollars and fifty-eight cents. In one month, I gave to foreign missions, ten cents, to the mite society, fifty cents, and twelve cents to the Five Points Mission, in New York. I wasn't living here then, of course, but I suppose I thought the Mission needed money. These little contributions of mine were not large, but they brought me into direct contact with church work, and that has been a benefit to me all my life. It is a mistake for a man to think that he must be rich to help others."

TEN THOUSAND DOLLARS

He earned and saved ten thousand dollars before he was twenty-five years old.

Before he attained his majority, Rockefeller formed a partnership with another young man named Hewett, and began a warehouse and produce business. This was the natural outgrowth of his freight clerkship on the docks. In five years, he had amassed about ten thousand dollars besides earning a reputation for business capacity and probity.

HE REMEMBERED THE OIL

He never forgot those experiments with the crude oil.

Discoveries became more and more frequent in the Pennsylvania oil territory. There was a rush of speculators to the new land of fortune. Men owning impoverished farms suddenly found themselves rich.

Thousands of excited men bid wildly against each other for newly-shot wells, paying fabulous sums occasionally for dry holes.

KEEPING HIS HEAD

John D. Rockefeller looked the entire field over carefully and calmly. Never for a moment did he lose his head. His Cleveland bankers and business friends had asked him to purchase some wells, if he saw fit, offering to back him up with $75,000 for his own investment [he was worth about $10,000 at the time], and to put in $400,000 more on his report.

The business judgment of this young man at twenty-five was so good, that his neighbors were willing to invest half a million dollars at his bidding.

He returned to Cleveland without investing a dollar. Instead of joining the mad crowd of producers, he sagaciously determined to begin at the other end of the business,—the refining of the product.

THERE WAS MORE MONEY IN A REFINERY

Among Rockefeller's acquaintances in Cleveland was one of these men. His name was Samuel Andrews. He had worked in a distillery, and was familiar with the process. He believed that there was a great business to be built up by removing the gases from the crude oil and making it safe for household use. Rockefeller listened to him, and became convinced that he was right. Here was a field as wide as the world, limited only by the production of crude oil. It was a proposition on which he could figure and make sure of the result. It was just the thing Rockefeller had been looking for. He decided to leave the production of oil to others, and to devote his attention to preparing it for market.

Andrews was a brother commission merchant. The two started a refinery, each closing out his former business connection. In two weeks, it was running night and day to fill orders. So great was the demand, and so great was the judgment of young Rockefeller,—seeing what no one else had seen.

A second refinery had to be built at once, and in two years their plants were turning out two thousand barrels of refined petroleum per day. Henry M. Flagler, already wealthy, came into the firm, the name of which then became Rockefeller, Flagler and Andrews. More refineries were built, not only at Cleveland, but also at other advantageous points. Competing refineries were bought or rendered ineffective by the cutting of prices.

It is related that Mr. Andrews became one day dissatisfied, and he was asked,—"What will you take for your interest?" Andrews wrote carelessly on a piece of paper,—"One million dollars." Within twenty-four hours he was handed that amount; Mr. Rockefeller saying,— "Cheaper at one million than ten." In building up the refinery business Rockefeller was the head; the others were the hands. He was always the general commanding, the tactician. He made the plans and his associates carried them out. Here was the post for which he had fitted himself, and in which his genius for planning had full sway. In the conduct of the refinery affairs, as in every enterprise in which he has taken part, he exemplified another rule to which he had adhered from his boyhood days. He was the leader in whatever he undertook. In going into any undertaking, John D. Rockefeller has made it his rule to have the chief authority in his own hands or to have nothing to do with the matter.

STANDARD OIL

In 1870, when Mr. Rockefeller was thirty-two years old, the business was merged into the Standard Oil Company, starting with a capital of one million dollars. Other pens have written the later story of that great corporation; how it started pipe lines to carry the oil to the seaboard; how it earned millions in by-products which had formerly run to waste; how it covered the markets of the world in its keen search for trade, distancing all competition, and cheapening its own processes so that its dividends in one year, 1899, amounted to $23,000,000 in excess of the fixed dividend upon the whole capital stock. This is the outcome of thirty years' development. The corporation is now the greatest business combination of modern times, or of any age of the world. Mr. Rockefeller's annual income from his holdings of Standard Oil stock is estimated at about sixteen millions of dollars.

MR. ROCKEFELLER'S PERSONALITY

The brains of all this, the owner of the largest percentage of the stock in the parent corporation, and in most of the lesser ones, is now sixty-two years old. His personality is simple and unaffected, his tastes domestic, and the trend of his thoughts decidedly religious. His Cleveland residential estate is superb, covering a large tract of park-like land,—but even there he has shown his unselfishness by donating a large portion of his land to the city for park purposes. His New York home is not a pretentious place,—solid, but by no means elegant in outward appearance. Between the two homes he divides his time with his wife and children. He is an earnest and hardworking member of the Fifth Avenue Baptist Church, in New York, and does much to promote the good work carried on by that organization. He is particularly interested in the Sunday-school work.

AT THE OFFICE

He arises early in the morning, at his home, and, after a light breakfast, attends to some of his personal affairs there. He is always early on hand at the great Standard Oil building on lower Broadway, New York, and, during the day, he transacts business connected with the management of that vast corporation. There is hardly one of our business men of whom the public at large knows so little. He avoids publicity as most men would the plague. The result is that he is the only one of our very wealthy men who maintains the reputation of being different from the ordinary run of mortals. To most newspaper readers, he is a man of mystery, a sort of financial wizard who sits in his office and heaps up wealth after the fashion of Aladdin and other fairy-tale heroes.

All this is wide of the mark. It would be hard to find a more commonplace, matter-of-fact man than John D. Rockefeller. His tall form, with the suggestion of a stoop in it, his pale, thoughtful face and reserved manner, suggest the scholar or professional man rather than an industrial Hercules or a Napoleon of finance. He speaks in a slow, deliberate manner, weighing each word. There is nothing impulsive or bombastic about him. But his conversation impresses one as consisting of about one hundred per cent. of cold, compact, boiled-down common sense.

Here is to be noted one characteristic of the great oil magnate which has helped to make him what he is. The popular idea of a multi-millionaire is a man who has taken big risks, and has come out luckily. He is a living refutation of this conception. He is careful and cautious by nature, and he has made these traits habitual for a lifetime; he conducts all his affairs on the strictest business principles.

FORESIGHT

The qualities which have made him so successful are largely those which go to the making of any successful business man,—industry, thrift, perseverance, and foresight. Three of these qualities would have made him a rich man; the last has distinguished him as the richest man. One of his business associates said of him, the other day:—

"I believe the secret of his success, so far as there is any secret, lies in power of foresight, which often seems to his associates to be wonderful. It comes simply from his habit of looking at every side of a question, of weighing the favorable and unfavorable features of a situation, and of sifting out the inevitable result through his unfailing good judgment."

This is his own personal statement, put into other words, so it may be accepted as true. The encouraging part of it is that, while such foresight as Rockefeller displays may be ascribed partly to natural endowment, both he and his friend say that it is more largely a matter of habit, made effective by continual practice.

HYGIENE

At noon he takes a very simple lunch at his club, or at some downtown restaurant. The lunch usually consists of a bowl of bread and milk. He remains at the office until late in the afternoon, and before dinner he takes some exercise. In winter, he skates when possible. And at other seasons of the year, he nearly always drives in the park or on the avenues. Mr. Rockefeller has great faith in fresh air as a tonic.

AT HOME

The evenings are nearly always spent at home, for neither Mr. Rockefeller nor any of the children are fond of "society," as the word is understood in New York. The children seem to have inherited many of their father's sensible ideas, and John D. Rockefeller, Jr., has apparently escaped the fate of most rich men's sons. He has a deep sense of responsibility as the heir-apparent to so much wealth; and, since his graduation from college, he has devoted himself to a business career, starting at the bottom and working upward, step by step. It is now generally known that he has been very successful in his business ventures, and he bids fair to become a worthy successor to his father. He is now actively engaged in important philanthropic enterprises in New York. Miss Bessie became the wife of a poor clergyman of the Baptist Church in Cleveland; while Miss Alta is married to a prominent young business man in Chicago.

PHILANTHROPY

Mr. Rockefeller has during many years turned over to his children a great many letters from needy people, asking them to exercise their own judgment in distributing charities.

While he has himself given away millions for education and charity, he would have given more were it not for his dread of seeming ostentatious. But he never gives indiscriminately, nor out of hand. When a charity appeals to him, he investigates it thoroughly, just as he would a business scheme. If he decides that its object is worthy, he gives liberally; otherwise, not a cent can be got out of him.

It may be imagined that such a man is busy to the full limit of his working capacity. This is true. He is too busy for any of the pastimes and pleasures in which most wealthy men seek diversion. He is thoroughly devoted to his home and family, and spends as much as possible of his time with them. He is a man who views life seriously, but in his quiet way he can get as much enjoyment out of a good story or a meeting with an old friend as can any other man.

PERSEVERANCE

When I asked Mr. Rockefeller what he considers has most helped him in obtaining success in business, he answered: "It was early training, and the fact that I was willing to persevere. I do not think there is any other quality so essential to success of any kind as the quality of perseverance. It overcomes almost everything, even nature."

It is to be said of his business enterprises, looking at them in a large way, that he has given to the world good honest oil, of standard quality; that his employees are always well paid; that he has given away more money in benevolence than any other business man in America. And everything about the man indicates that he is likely to "persevere" in the course he has so long pursued, turning his vast wealth into institutes for public service.

A GENIUS FOR MONEY MAKING

"There are men born with a genius for money-making," says Mathews. "They have the instinct of accumulation.

The talent and the inclination to convert dollars into doubloons by bargains or shrewd investments are in them just as strongly marked and as uncontrollable as were the ability and the inclination of Shakespeare to produce Hamlet and Othello, of Raphael to paint his cartoons, of Beethoven to compose his symphonies, or Morse to invent an electric telegraph. As it would have been a gross dereliction of duty, a shameful perversion of gifts, had these latter disregarded the instincts of their genius and engaged in the scramble for wealth, so would a Rothschild, an Astor, and a Peabody have sinned had they done violence to their natures, and thrown their energies into channels where they would have proved dwarfs and not giants."

The opportunity which came to young Rockefeller does not occur many times in many ages: and in a generous interpretation of his opportunity, he has already invested a great deal of his earnings in permanently useful philanthropies.